MAN,
LISTEN
to your
WOMAN

A.J. BEECH

CREATION
HOUSE PRESS
A STRANG COMPANY

MAN, LISTEN TO YOUR WOMAN by Alton J. Beech
Published by Creation House Press
A Strang Company
600 Rinehart Road
Lake Mary, FL 32746
www.creationhouse.com

Unless otherwise noted all Scripture quotations are from the Holy Bible, New International Version. Copyright © 1973, 1978, 1984, International Bible Society.
Used by permission.

Scripture quotations marked KJV are from the King James Version of the Bible.

Cover design by Judith McKittrick

Interior design by Candace Ziegler

Library of Congress Control Number: 2003106693

International Standard Book Number: 1-59185-240-4

This book is dedicated to my lovely wife and our four beautiful children. Thanks also to The Greater Anointing Harvest Church family and all the special people in my life who helped make this book possible.

ACKNOWLEDGMENTS

First, I would like to thank my Lord and Savior, Jesus Christ, who is the head of my life. I believe God inspired me to write this book because its message is very much needed in this hour.

I also would like to thank the love of my life, my lovely wife, Tina, who has been an example for me and who has encouraged me to continue to pursue the Lord's work. I also want to thank my four beautiful children for their love and support and The Greater Anointing Harvest Church family for supporting me in my endeavors.

CONTENTS

PREFACE

My prayer and hope is that both men and women will see themselves between the lines of this book and catch the wisdom within these pages. I certainly do not speak for all men, but this issue is close to my heart. I have had to learn the art of listening myself, and it is that process of discovery that I have to offer you here.

As you have probably noticed by now, this book is titled *Man, Listen to Your Woman*, not *Man, Listen to Women*. This is because it is important for a man to listen to his own woman. Not just any woman or women in general, but to the woman he has wed in the covenant of marriage. I could have phrased this to read that a man should listen to his own wife, but I chose not to phrase the title in this way because of the tendency for men to think they should have the benefits of ownership over their wives. I steered away from even hinting at this concept because a man will surely run into trouble if he thinks he owns his wife or if acts like he does. While it is true that the wife belongs to her husband, it is also true that the husband belongs to his wife. This belonging does not mean that either of them has the right to mistreat the other in the way that a person who owns a car has the right to mistreat or ignore the maintenance needs of his or her car.

While you may agree with the statement I made above, if you are like many people of both today and yesterday, you may still be holding to the idea that a man's gender entitles him to own his wife or treat her accordingly. Or what a man has and is proud of—a prized son or daughter, a good paying job, a fine car—gives him this right. Or a man's frustrations about what he does not have or his feelings of inadequacy give him the right to exert his manhood over his wife and dominate her in a way that wounds her.

On the surface you may feel that you don't in any way hold to these ideas, but on some level you may actually be living your life in a way that reflects otherwise. My hope is that areas where you are failing to respect your wife if you are a man, or are failing to think you deserve respect if you are a woman, will be uncovered and healed. My prayer is that you will gain and learn how to better express respect for your mate, for yourself, and for others.

As you explore how men are not superior to women just like women are not superior to men, and as you see in more concrete ways that men do not own women and do not have the right to behave as though they do, I am sure that you will begin to take responsibility for cherishing and honoring one another in ways that will enrich your marriage and everyone around you. While the title of this book seems to indicate that it is a book for a men only, this actually is not the case because women have a responsibility in this too. As author Joshua Harris said in his book *I Kissed Dating Goodbye,* a woman should not give a man any reason to think he owns her.[1]

I am confident that your journey in discovering the hidden treasures that can only be discovered through speaking into one another's lives in new and deeper ways will cause you to fall in love with this subject as much as my wife and I have.

INTRODUCTION

When you first picked up this book and read the title, you may have thought I would be contradicting the scripture that clearly tells us that women should submit to their own husbands, as unto Christ. My purpose, however, is to do the very opposite of that. Instead, I would like to take a closer look at that scripture—Ephesians 5:22—within the context of the Scripture just before it. In Ephesians 5:21, we are told that men and women should submit to one another in the fear of God. And so, if we examine these two scriptures together we see that, yes, a woman should listen to her man...but we also see that a man should listen to his woman. How else can a marital relationship be successful? Without mutual respect, a marriage is sure to be a hazardous mine field for both parties rather than the garden of delight that God intended it to be!

One of the hazards in a marriage that lacks mutual respect as described in Ephesians 21-22 is poor communication. Rather than recognizing and benefiting from the strengths that each person is able to bring to the marriage, the two become so frustrated with one another that they become overwhelmed with nitpicking and fault finding. This downward spiral often results in a failed marriage simply because the man drains his wife of her strength and her ability to express love and function in spiritually, physically and emotionally healthy ways.

If only more men understood the importance of complimenting their wives and remembering to say those sweet little nothings that mean so much to a woman.

Because a woman's strength is in her sensitivity, it is very hard for a woman to function sexually, emotionally and mentally without consistently being encouraged by her mate. Just like a car cannot run without gas, a woman needs to be showered with words of affirmation, affection and love. If a woman is forced to run on empty for too long, she may begin to contemplate separation or divorce. Unfortunately, until they are shaken to the core by the threat of a looming divorce, some men will drain their wives empty by failing to give them consideration (see 1 Peter 3:7). Why would any man deny his wife the respect she deserves (and the Bible demands) until his wife and marriage are so bone dry that both are nearly lifeless? Why wouldn't a man want his wife and marriage to flourish in an environment of mutual love *and* respect?

As you read this book, I am confident it will become clear that two-way communication is both a God-given benefit and a God-given necessity for the husband and the wife. Without mutual respect that is demonstrated by speaking and listening to one another, the wife runs on empty because her needs are not met and the husband is weighted down because he is unnecessarily carrying the weight of a failing marriage and not benefiting from his wife's insightfulness, watchfulness, and sensitivities.

Taking a deeper look at how these two scriptures work together and then taking steps toward building one another up will affect others as well. The garden of mutual respect will be a place of rest where the children will learn and grow from their parents' examples. People in their church and community will be encouraged by the wife, who glows in the knowledge that her husband values her mind as well as her body, and by the husband, who walks peacefully and yet tall because he is considerately giving *and* receiving. As this husband and wife fuel one another by their mutual love and respect, they will bring warmth and light to others.

Are you a man who has a hard time listening to your wife? Or are you a woman who feels she isn't being heard? If so, this book is for you. There is no need to continue running on empty and being weighted down by the unnecessary burden of doing it alone. You can be warmed and filled; you can be a brighter light to the world, together.

1

THE FINE ART OF LISTENING

Pay attention. This is for your own good. While it is true that this book is not just about men listening to their wives, I will venture to say that the welfare of our families, churches and communities would improve dramatically if husbands and wives would begin to speak into one another's lives freely and regularly. The fruit of those two-way exchanges would enhance hearts, homes, and communities in innumerable ways. But where does this mutual respect and two-way communication that would so enhance all of our lives begin? With humility before God—in many cases with men exhibiting that humility in their relationships with their wives.

Two-way communication is a form of giving and receiving attention in a way that expresses humility before God and man. As we explore this further, I am confident that your desire to be a better listener will grow, and you will be eager to put your discoveries into practice. Rather than providing you with a step-by-step plan of give and take that takes the form of some kind of manipulative formula, I will be digging out nuggets of truth from the Scripture and sharing my heart with you.

The first nugget of truth for us to examine is just how important it is for a man to be considerate to his wife and treat her with respect. Even if you already know where I am going with this, you will benefit from contemplating the fact that husbands who do not give their wives proper attention are not only hurting their wives, but they are also hurting themselves and others because they will not get the attention they desire from God. How do we know this? Because 1 Peter 3:7 tells us, "Husbands, in the same way be considerate as you live with your wives, and treat them with respect as the weaker partner and as heirs with you of the gracious gift of life, so that nothing will hinder your prayers."

The bottom line here is that a man's prayers will be hindered if he doesn't treat that woman of his right! Second Chronicles 7:14 makes this point in another way by saying that if God's people would, first off, humble themselves and pray, He would hear from heaven and heal our land. Both of these scriptures show us the link between answered prayers and humility. With this link in mind, it is clear that we need to know the truth about whether or not we are really humble—or just assume that we are. A good barometer of this is right in our own homes, in how we treat one another. In the case of the man, his relationship with his own wife will probably tell the true tale of just how humble he really is.

In the case of the single man or woman who probably hopes to be married someday, there are still plenty of opportunities in your daily life for you to practice keeping your pride, stubbornness and temper in check so that you will be exhibiting humility now and will exhibit in other ways in the future.

My point here is that when a man refuses to listen to his spouse, he is keeping his marriage in a weak state, damaging his relationship with God and handicapping the effectiveness of his prayers and ministry. Of course, listening is much more than just the hearing of words. What is she is trying to say to me? Do I really understand her meaning? Does she have more to say that I need to invite her to express? If questions like these do not come to a man's mind when his wife is expressing her heart to him, it is time for him to prayerfully examine the reasons why he is not actively listening to her.

There is a vast array of different possibilities of why a man may have trouble taking his wife's ideas into consideration. It may be because he is afraid that not being the sole provider and boss over every situation will somehow emasculate them, make him less of a man. It may be because he is afraid that he will look like less of a hero to his wife or to others who may be in hearing distance. I mention these reasons because they are more common than most of us would like to admit. Why? Because they are all related to pride, to lack of humility.

I have chosen to cut right to the heart of this matter immediately because humility is such an important part of a man's life, and the lack of it will result in such severe ramifications. As we examined earlier, if the way a man treats his wife is not marked by respect and humility, his prayers will be hindered. I will venture to say that he will actually be less effective as a man because he is not benefiting from all that God has intended for his wife to add to his life. So many men are unnecessarily crippled by an inability or unwillingness to listen to their wives, to treat them respectfully. They are handicapped because they do not realize that they would actually be empowered and enhanced in their leadership in their homes and in their communities if they would welcome and seek out the advice of the woman that God has placed in their lives to help them. They are handicapped because they have not allowed their lives to complete them in the way God intended.

While it may be true that active listening—paying attention to, considering, and asking questions about what is being said—may not come naturally to most of us, with a lifetime of practice and mutual respect, a man and a woman who are yoked together in this expression of love can develop this art in such a way that they are richly and beautifully synchronized in every area of their lives.

2

WHAT DOES LISTENING HAVE TO DO WITH AUTHORITY?

ere's a thought to keep in mind: Listening can keep trouble away. Listening can help you fulfill your role. Good listeners make good role models.

Most of us have heard that communication is important in any relationship, but too many people do not take this seriously. They do not truly realize how critical it is to have good, open lines of communication in their families. One sure way to discourage open communication is to refuse to listen to the other party. People who are good listeners build relationships by just listening, and they are better able to respond to the needs of others because they know what those needs are.

Because men are the heads of their households, many often feel they have no reason to give ear to whatever suggestions their wives offer—even if that advice is beneficial to their families. They think their presence in the home is enough to serve and support their families.

But men, consider this. Our children learn what they live. They are aware of and react to the way we parents listen and interact with each other. Our children are very keen on the manner in which they respond to their mothers. The manner in which we communicate says a lot about whether or not we truly honor and respect women. Thus, how we treat our spouses shows a great deal about ourselves. It tells how much we respect and love ourselves

5

(see Ephesians 5:28–29).

Women, of course, should not be exempt from considering this either. Our communication sets a tone in the home. The refusal to listen, and the stubbornness and pride that accompany it, may very well be something—at least in part—that our children are learning from us. Since the attitudes and behaviors that our children learn at home will shape how they interact with others today and in the future—including teachers, law officers and other authority figures—our children need us to provide them with models of how and why it is important to communicate with others in a respectful, cooperative and often compliant way. If our children do not see us responding to one another in a way that honors God, they will tend to relate to their teachers, law officers and other authority figures in a less than honorable way.

Although the consequences for failing to listen stretch beyond our marriages and out to our children, many couples fail to be careful and mindful about what their children are hearing and seeing, and even allow a lack of listening to turn into something rather ugly right in front of the children. However, much conflict, either in front of children or not, could easily be avoided if the husband and wife were working together as a team and diligently looking for ways to strengthen that team.

When the husband-wife team is flowing together, other needs of the children are met as well. This is true because children often need their mothers to speak to their fathers on their behalf. Because children generally spend more time with their mothers than with their fathers, the mother is usually more up-to-date on what is going on in their children lives. Many times the mother is more aware and attentive to the needs of the children than the father is even when the father lives in the same household and the mother works. When the mother sees that her child's needs are changing, are not being met or are being met by an unhealthy source, she will often speak to the father on behalf of the children.

But what happens if the father is in the habit of not listening to his wife? The needs of the child will often go unmet or the mother will become overwhelmed because she is constantly trying to fill in the gaps where the father is not stepping in to help where help is needed. The message to the children is a dangerous one because it conveys that the father does not care about the needs of the children and does not respect his wife's input. Both of these messages point to a lack of humility before God and a failure to honor God by providing for the needs of the family.

We have already discussed how this failure to provide the children with the role model of humility will spill over into the children's relationships with others. It will have other ramifications as well, including frustration for the wife and children. Also, because women are so giving, they will often try to make up for their husband's lack and end up suffering burnout. This is especially true for the vast majority of mothers who have grown accustomed to giving of themselves, so used to doing so much, for so long, that they end up giving every ounce of their energy and attention to their families that they neglect themselves and fail to ask for help. I have to wonder how many husbands have no clue how many times their wives have thought about asking for more assistance in certain areas but have said to themselves, *Aw, just forget it. I'll go ahead and do it myself.* More than likely, these women gave up on asking for help long ago or have gotten the unspoken message from their husbands that help simply is not available or deserved.

I believe that a lot of husbands would have to admit that they have sidestepped taking responsibility for their wives' burnout with justifications like, "Well, whose fault is it if she doesn't communicate those things to me? All she has to do is ask for help." But like most people, I have observed a tendency for husbands to take advantage of their wives' tendency to give until she is completely spent of all energy and other personal resources. Think about it. Many husbands avoid doing what is the glaringly obvious right thing to do. They fail to assist even though the need for help has not been verbally expressed, or to invite and encourage everyone in the family to ask for help when it is needed, or to pitch in even when it does not appear to be needed.

A humble and attentive listener will be paying close attention to both spoken and unspoken messages—and will respond to them quickly. A child who sees this kind of humility in the home will learn by example of how to respond in this way in his or her relationships with others.

3

SELECTIVE HEARING:
THE NAG VS. THE IGNORER

"All she does is complain, complain, complain." How many times have you heard some husband say that of his wife? Interestingly, most wives would probably say something like: "He never listens. If I could only get him to listen..." I believe many of the men who say their wives nag them a lot have made a habit of ignoring their spouses. This can be a very vicious cycle—the husband ignores his wife because he doesn't want to hear her nag him and complain, and the wife nags and complains because her husband doesn't listen. It has to end somewhere. Someone has to give up!

4

FROM WHENCE COMETH YOUR LISTENING HABITS?

Monkey see, monkey do. That's a concept we heard as children, but there is a lot of truth in those four little words. Oftentimes the manner in which men listen to their wives is adopted from how they have seen their fathers interact with their mothers or how they observed men treating women in general. Every man is different, but many men, perhaps subconsciously, manage to choose spouses who are much like their mothers.

For men whose mothers are very assertive women, used to taking control of the household for one reason or another, having a wife with similar characteristics can be challenging. The man may like the fact that, like his mother, his mate always has suggestions and comes up with a lot of ideas and plans. However, after he has been married for a while he may grow to resent those traits, thinking his wife is treating him like a child. If he does not communicate his feelings about this to his spouse, anger and resentment will build up in his heart and bitterness will fester.

Understanding some of the why's behind how we are feeling and responding will also help rid of us of bitterness that has taken root over time. This is particularly important because many of us do not come from healthy, stable homes. One or perhaps both of our parents may have been abusive or neglectful.

If you are like most people, pondering whether your spouse's manner reminds you of how a parent treated you will help you see the real root of your marital conflict or frustration. Again, communication with your spouse is key here because even a few slight adjustments in your spouse's approach and tone can make a world of difference. Or it could be that once you recognize that you have been responding to how you feel about how your parent treated you rather than to what your spouse is actually doing or saying, you will more clearly see that your spouse's motives are really not as bad as you once thought they were.

Recognizing now how your innermost areas of hurt and vulnerability have been clouding your ability to hear clearly and responding in a gentle and helpful way will help you break the cycle of hurt in your family and replace it with a free and steady flow of blessing one another in the spirit of unity that will spill out on others now and in the years to come.

5

JUST WHAT DOES IT MEAN FOR A HUSBAND TO SUBMIT?

Most people, at first glance, have a hard time swallowing the idea of submission. Of course, it is easy for husbands to swallow the idea of their wives submitting to them (Eph. 5:22). But the context of that scripture, that they too must submit to their wives because couples are called to submit to one another in the fear of the Lord, is not as easy for most men to accept. (Eph. 5:21). Hard as it may be though, one scripture cannot be taken out of the context of the other and the man must humble himself and submit whether it is comfortable for him at first or not.

Where does submitting to one another begin? It is easy to see that it begins with listening to one another. Why? Because it is not possible to submit to someone without first identifying what he or she is suggesting or requesting. When couples demonstrate mutual respect through listening to one another and then submitting to one another, they show a reverence for God and receive the benefits of doing so. On the one hand, they enjoy the positive results of doing things the best way, God's way. Plus, they receive the benefits of His favor being more freely at work in their lives.

A doorway to blessing and favor

Unfortunately, many homes lack this blessing and favor because they lack the order of the husband and wife communicating genuinely and submitting to one another wholeheartedly. In many homes, the lack extends even further because the woman's need to talk goes unmet. If the husband fails to meet his wife's need for the relief and comfort she would receive if he would talk with her regularly, then she will oftentimes become overwhelmed with feelings of loneliness. Consequently, her burnout from carrying too much of the needs of the household is further complicated by her feelings of isolation.

If you asked the average wife to describe the most important thing she needs from her husband, she would probably say she needs him to listen to her and truly care about what is upon her heart. As you contemplate the number of women who are weeping, overcome with loneliness, because their husbands won't listen to them, I encourage you, my brother, to ask yourself if your wife is one of them.

Over the years I have counseled many married women who were seeking help because their husbands had failed to give them the listening ear they needed and some of their issues had remained critical and unresolved. In many cases they probably would not have needed counsel from me if they had been able to express themselves to their husbands and to be heard by them.

The truth of the matter is that two-way communication is one of a women's basic needs. Many of the men who wonder why their wives are always on the phone with a female friend do not realize that their own failure to listen to what is on their wives' hearts is what is leading them to pour their hearts out to someone else, to someone who will show them the consideration of listening.

A top priority

I believe some men are afraid to sit and talk with their

wives because they fear the conversation will never end. Each day when I come home I try to devote twenty minutes of listening attentively as my wife tells me about the highlights of her day. Why twenty minutes? Because that is my capacity for listening to her when I first get home. Unlike some men who can give their wives undivided attention for hours at a time right away, I have to work hard at listening—especially right after I get home. While this was a discipline at first, I have gained a true appreciation for how a woman can express her feelings, what she likes and what she doesn't like.

I have also grown to appreciate how a woman simply wants someone to be attentive to her as she shares her thoughts and experiences. I have learned to even love how she doesn't always make sense, and seems to talk in circles a bit, but always feels so much better after she has shared what is on her heart and mind.

Because it is difficult for me to listen to my wife for a long period of time right after I come home in the evening, I have found other ways and times to set aside quality time with her. I always try to make it a point to call her several times throughout the day, even if it is just to say hello. We usually get to sit and talk one to two hours each night before we go to bed, and when I travel we set a schedule of when we will talk with each other.

You may be thinking that I am quite the husband, but the truth of the matter is that I was not the one who came up with these ways to communicate often and stay close to one another. My wife was actually the one who suggested we do all of these things, and because I have listened to and followed through with her suggestions, our relationship grows stronger throughout each day. With effort and self-discipline, I have learned to manage my responsibilities in a way that gives first priority to my relationship with God and with my wife. With practice, submitting to my wife and fulfilling my responsibility to listen to her has become easier and more enjoyable for me.

A responsibility, not just an afterthought

From my own experience, I know that a man runs from his responsibility to communicate with his wife is only making things harder for himself. On the surface, avoiding the discipline of being a good listener seems like the easy way out, but in the long run the reverse is true. In Genesis 1 we read that when God created man, He gave Adam everything he needed and in return, the man was responsible for giving the woman what she needed.

When a man fails to live up this responsibility, he is hurting himself as well as his wife. Remember, Eve came from Adam's side. In Genesis 2:18, we read that God created the woman for the man as a suitable helper. If a man only sees this help as cooking and cleaning, and does not allow her to help him in other ways, he will lack in his life. In essence, if a man does not allow his wife to do what God created her to do in his life, he will not be a complete man. Take for instance the man who cannot handle his family's finances very well. Some men can make the money, but they cannot save it. If that man's wife knows how to save and budget, they would be better off financially if he did not plow ahead on his own, too proud to welcome her assistance.

Even though I am a pastor of a congregation, I am not exempt from listening to my wife. If I do not continue in my efforts to learn how to listen to my wife, I will find myself incomplete and out of balance. For example, I would have quite unbalanced view of myself if I only listened to what people say to my face. Over time I have learned that while people often compliment me on my strengths, they may be saying something very different behind my back. Because she is my helpmate, my wife has the unique position of being able to tell me the truth about what she sees in me. I would hate to see how egotistic I might become if only I listened to all the people who tell me how awesome they think I am. Fortunately, God sometimes uses my wife to pop my expanding bubble a bit when she points out something I needed to hear about myself. She is the balance of my scale.

Don't get me wrong, my wife also compliments me, strokes my ego and tells me wonderful things about myself. However, her loving words of wisdom, correction and criticism have brought out practicality, reality and balance in my life. I'm not saying that is always easy or always has been, but I can easily say that when I stopped ignoring my wife and began to truly listen to her, I started to see a wonderful transformation in my life that included my seeing how dysfunctional my upbringing was and how that had impeded me from receiving what all that God had intended for her to add to my life.

A sign of maturity

Now, when it comes to listening to her, I take the bitter with the sweet. I wouldn't be a real man if I could only accept her compliments. We can see this same principle in operation when we consider our relationship with God. Wouldn't we question the maturity in a Christian man's walk if he wholeheartedly welcomed "atta boy" revelations from God, but stubbornly ignored correction, rebuke and warning from Him? This tendency can be seen when people are quick to believe that God is speaking to them when the message seems to affirm them, but slow to acknowledge the possibility that God is speaking to them when the message points to a need for correction.

Just as a Christian believer will be handicapped by selectively hearing only what they wanted to hear from God, a man is handicapped when he will only hear those things from his wife that will stroke his ego. I know that I have become a more complete man now that I have started to work on those areas of weakness that God and my wife point out. I can now honestly say that I am no longer just half a man. I am now becoming a whole, complete man.

I fully recognize that as I listen to my wife and allow the ways of excellence in her life to speak to (and yes, minister to) the areas where I was lacking, I am becoming more and more complete. Because I have experienced this healing and revolutionary change myself, my hope is that other men will enjoy the benefits of this kind of restoration.

Why would a man continue to be bull headed just because he is the head of the house? Isn't it the woman who nourishes and shapes the home? But, if the man has a pit bull attitude, it will be harder for the woman to help him, resulting in him unnecessarily handicapping himself. His lack of maturity will be sure to be a constant source of lack, and often harm, to everyone around him.

A safeguard

There is another danger as well: When a man is not open to listening to his wife, it will be easier for him to listen to another woman. This is true because a man's true strength lies in a woman's softness, love, compassion, sensitivity, emotion and balance. The man who is not allowing his wife to complete him will tend to begin looking for it elsewhere.

Some men are able to receive from another woman but not from his wife because at home his ego has him wrapped up in ruling his roost all by himself. With another woman, he does not have the same ego attachment to being in a position of household domination.

Look at Abraham, both his strength and what I call a man's ego. In Genesis 16, we read that Abraham's wife, Sarah, became weary of waiting on God's promise that she would have a baby. She thought she simply could not bear a child because she was well along in years. She suggested that Abraham could take her maid Hagar as his wife in order for her to give Abraham an heir. Abraham gladly listened to his wife.

Things were quite different when Sarah saw her mistake and she wanted Abraham to put Hagar out. This time he refused to listen (see Genesis 21:8–13). It was not until God spoke to him—reminding him that the promise to make Abraham a great nation would come through Isaac and not Ishmael—that Abraham honored Sarah's request.

Sarah was not saint in all of this, and her motivation for wanting Hagar and her son put out may not have been pure. But she realized before her husband did that his two sons should be separated. There will be many times in a husband's life when his wife will become aware of a need before he sees it. A man can be aware of a lot of things, especially when he is moving under the anointing. But women tend to be sensitive naturally. You can put a woman in a dark room with a blindfold on, and she can tell you what is in that room before the light comes on. She can tell the man which women to watch out for in a minute, because she was born with built-in radar. She can warn a man about hidden dangers before they become evident to him.

A man who is being completed by his wife and responding to her warnings about potential dangers ahead will be much more likely to sidestep temptation long before it has a chance to knock very loudly. However, if he has selective hearing and only takes her advice when it suits his ego or desires, he is headed for trouble.

A learning process

If we look at what happened as a result of Abraham taking Sarah's advice, we see an example of why some men are afraid to listen to their wives. They have read the few examples in Scripture of men who listened to women and were steered in the wrong direction. This pitfall is again the result of taking a scriptural account out of the context of the rest of Scripture. A man's conclusion is faulty if he relies on isolated examples to bring him to the conclusion that he should not engage in a mutually sub-missive relationship with his spouse. If we are to consider examples of poor advice in light of other accounts, we would also find several examples of women who gave great counsel to men, causing the situation to turn out well. For example, Esther helped to free her people; Deborah was a judge; King Naaman's servant girl per-suaded him to listen to the prophet Elisha, and he was healed (see 2 Kings 5); and Abigail, the wife of the foolish Nabal, stopped David from shedding innocent blood (see 1 Samuel 25:32–35).

In a mutually supportive, cooperative relationship, both the husband and wife are giving their input and do their best to make decisions that are based on sound judg-ment, prayer, and wise counsel. A good woman would not seek to destroy her man. She would seek to build him up because she is his helper. Yes, the partners will make some mistakes, but they will have made them together and will learn from them together.

If we return to our example of Sarah, we see that she did recognize the error of her original suggestion. Does that mean that all of her advice for the rest of Abraham's life should be ignored? Of course not. Does the fact that Sarah gave Abraham poor advice mean that no man should ever listen to his own wife? Of course not.

A source of comfort

Whatever his reasoning, a man will suffer unnecessarily if he is not receiving the benefits of listening to his wife. Part of his suffering will be the ramifications of his wife's suffering. Once, I was driving with a married couple that seemed to be happy and have a good marriage. But when I mentioned the title of this book to them, the beautiful woman went from being pleasant to unpleasant as she turned her head in her husband's direction. She asked me how she might get a copy of the book. For the rest of the journey, it was as if we were flying through turbulence on an airplane; the environment in the car had changed from pleasant to volatile.

This was obviously an area that had been causing this woman much suffering. As I listened to her express her pain in a number of ways, I began to think about how so many women suffer from depression, pop pills and visit the doctor about stress-related illnesses—all because their spouses won't listen to them. A lot of men think they are taking the easy way out by not living up to their responsibility to talk with their wives but don't realize that their wives' emotional pain is taking a toll on the whole family.

Many women feel as though they are trapped or wounded; they are looking for someone to share with, someone to hear them out after a long day. After she is finished dealing with everyone else, she now needs her man to listen to her. She wants to talk to him. She needs someone to look into her eyes and give her his undivided attention. But sadly, many women are trapped in severe depression because they are starving for their husband's attention and genuine concern.

If not changed, the spiral is downward for everyone. If a man's wife is not happy, then he will not be happy either. Failure to communicate is a shortcut, to be sure. It is a sure and quick road to discontent and havoc, not to the effective and energy management that so many men expect.

I do not buy into the idea that men have an excuse for not talking to their wives because men have short attention spans. I think this is probably true whenever the conversation is not about something that interests him. Most men could spend hours talking about sports, his car or truck, or his business.

Most men can remember a time when they were eager to hear anything and everything their women had to say to them. In fact, on their first date, these men probably made a great impression by being such a good listeners. They probably stayed attentive for hours on end while they talked on the phone with their potential mates. But then, after being married for a while, they suddenly are just not able to listen anymore? I don't buy it. To be honest, I believe most men listen to what they want to hear when they want to hear it.

How can any man be too busy to listen to his wife when she is hurting or concerned about the welfare of the family? However, when a woman doesn't make talking with her husband a priority, she will end up spilling the beans where a husband probably doesn't want them spilt—to his mother-in-law, for example. Many men make the mistake of getting angry and withdrawing even more when this happens. A man who is providing the support and comfort that a woman finds in sharing her heart will probably find that his beans are safe in his own cupboard.

A source of strength

I also don't buy into the idea that a man is showing weakness when he allows her to flow in her gifting and minister to him. In Mark 14:3–9, was it a sign of weakness when Jesus humbled Himself and let a former prostitute anoint His feet and head? No, it was a sign of strength. If Jesus's character led Him to accept ministry from a former prostitute, should not a husband look to this model and welcome his wife to recognize his needs and minister to him in her own unique ways?

Not only did Jesus accept Mary's ministry, He defended it before others. Speaking of this, Jesus said, "Leave her alone...Why are you bothering her? She has done a beautiful thing to me" (Mark 14:6). Jesus was not embarrassed by the fact that He had received ministry from a woman, was he?

A man who does not receive ministry from his wife is keeping her anointing shut up in her spirit. Many times the very thing that a man is praying for is waiting for him in his wife. Because of her sensitivities, the wife probably knows exactly what her husband needs. However, it will remain shut up in her until he is willing to receive God's provision through her.

Mary is an example of a woman who was sitting in the midst of a number of men who were not as sensitive to Jesus' needs as Mary was. I could share many examples from my own life of times when it was obvious that the woman in the situation was much more sensitive than the men. An example that is a little more glaring than some of the others took place on a Sunday afternoon when two of the church's deacons were sitting with me in my office taking care of some business. One of them had a broken finger and had been taking medicine to stop the pain, but it seemed to have been making him sicker. He lay back onto the sofa, as the other deacon and I continued to do what we were doing without paying him any attention.

When my wife came into the office, she noticed right away that the deacon was not feeling well, even though he did not mention anything to her. It wasn't that we men weren't concerned about what he was going through, but we were less than attentive to him. We could have responded to her in a way that exhibited a weakness of character. For example, we could have become embarrassed by the fact that she noticed something that we did not and attempted to cover up our embarrassment by regarding her suggestions as being an intrusion on our "important church business." That, my friend, would have appeared to be weak. The strong thing to do was to applaud her ability to see what we did not see.

Constant and consistent

While sensitivity to the needs of others is not as natural for a lot of men as it is for women, I think the lack of sensitivity is often as selective as a man's attention span. This selective attention can be seen in the number of men who suddenly become less attentive to their wives after the engagement and honeymoon are over. Prior to the marriage, the husbands were compassionate and sensitive, always eager to listen or help out when their then-girlfriends were going through difficult times. But then when the honeymoon is over, they can't even remember birthdays or anniversaries and opening car doors for their woman is a thing of the past. What happened? Selective attention.

While a man can benefit greatly from what his wife's

added sensitivities will bring to his life, gender differences do not excuse selective attention! Men certainly are still able to do the things that once made their wives feel loved and special. Their lack of consideration for their wives isn't related so much to their gender as it is to their degree of motivation. But all is not lost. Consistent expressions of being considerate and passionate can be restored. The honeymoon can begin again; the fires of romance can be rekindled.

A form of completion

Remember the couple I was riding with in the car? When his wife began to recommend that he read this book, the husband murmured. He feels like he doesn't listen to her because of the way she treats him.

After leaving the car I began to ponder what he had said, and then I thought about Proverbs 31:10–31, a passage that describes a virtuous woman. We focus on the virtuous woman so much that we fail to regard how complete a man her husband must have been. We always hear that "behind every good man, there is a good woman," but that goes both ways. Proverbs says that a good wife is the crown of her husband's head (see Proverbs 12:4). I believe that when a woman treats her husband well, it is easier for him to listen to her.

In Proverbs 31, the husband was famous wherever he went because of his wife's virtue. She opened her mouth with wisdom. This means that she was not restricted to doing the housework, but she knew how to talk to him, and if I might say, she knew how to stroke him. This is probably what made him comfortable enough to listen to her. He then helped to release his wife into her destiny. He was not intimidated by her success, as long as she was stroking him with her words of wisdom and helping with his direction.

Just imagine a woman speaking words of assurance to her husband. I'll just call him James for example. Picture his wife saying: "James, even though I have the ability to do all this work, I cannot do this well without your support. What is mine is yours. The attention you give me strengthens me to do what I do, and I will do my best to respect and obey you. I thank you for not being intimidated by my strength as a woman because you know that I am bone of your bone and flesh of your flesh. I thank you for listening with understanding. It helps me to carry myself with honor and not with a spirit of depression that would hinder me from carrying out my purpose."

This is an illustration of a very wise woman. Most men will not pay much attention to a negative or a double-minded woman. However, they will heed the advice of someone with the law of kindness coming out of her mouth instead of words that are bitter.

I believe it was the versatility of the virtuous woman that made her husband attentive to her needs. Let us look at the character of this woman. Most women are moved by their emotions and instincts, while most men are moved by what they see. If you cannot get your husband's attention, examine yourself and take a different approach. The woman in Proverbs 31 was independent, remained under authority and was faithful to her responsibility.

Furthermore, she worked willingly with her hands. She was a provider, rising early to do her work and considering a field and buying it. She was not wasteful. She was full of discernment, a confident woman, kind and unafraid to take chances. This virtuous woman carried herself well and wore the best clothes. She did things that would bring glory to her husband and not shame. She was creative, operating in purpose and moving in her destiny. She was not slothful.

Proverbs says, "He who finds a wife find what is good and receives favor from the Lord" (18:22). The phrase "receives favor from the Lord" implies that a wife is God-sent. It also suggests that God knows exactly what you need and that some of your destiny is wrapped up in your mate.

Men and women were intended to complement each other. Women have a spiritual sense keener than the nose of a bloodhound on a foxhunt. She can tell her husband who loves him and who despises him and who will be there for him and who won't. Because of our egos and go-get-it attitudes, we men often miss some things that are very important. This is why the woman is there to pick up what we have missed and communicate it back to us.

Too many men take a woman's strength for granted because she cannot lift 600 pounds. But she can carry a baby in her womb for nine months, which requires a different kind of strength. If that does not make any sense to you, then remember how God uses her emotions to balance us, to help remind us to be more compassionate and realize that we don't know everything and don't always have to be in control.

Women, though your husbands may seem bull-headed and insensitive sometimes, you can influence them to change. Just study 1 Peter 3. Read it carefully again and again, and ponder what it has to say. A believing wife can influence her husband for good without even saying a word.

Remember how the woman in Proverbs 31 opened her mouth with wisdom? Wisdom only reveals itself to those who are humble; because of her humility, a wise woman chooses her words carefully and thinks before she speaks. Her words are not careless; she is not always apologizing to her husband. The book of James says we should be quick to listen and slow to speak. Now that's a silent treatment that will work for a woman.

I am not talking about the carnal silent treatment that some women use against their husbands that does more harm than good; a wise woman will let the word of God operate though her emotions. Remember, James states that bitter and sweet water cannot come from the same fountain.

The right words, carefully spoken by a man's wife, can do wonders in a marriage. Some men who find it hard to listen have been in relationships that hurt, and they unconsciously bring that other relationship over into their marriages. Men are often as sensitive as women, and they need to know that they can trust their wives with their hurts. They need to know that their wives are not against them.

Woman of God, let your speech be always with grace, seasoned with salt, so you can minister to that husband of yours.

6

IS YOUR WIFE REALLY A NAG?

Women are not naggers, as many men think they are. To re-evaluate this, men must take a closer and more honest look at what they consider to be nagging. Men think their wives are nagging them when they ask questions such as: Did you forget to take out the trash again? Why didn't you let me know that you were working late? Why are you not spending more time with the kids? Why are you working so hard and have so little time for your family? Why did you forget my birthday and Mother's Day?

Most of the time the wife must remind her husband several times about his duties and responsibilities. Oftentimes, the man calls these reminders nagging, when in fact he is taking his wife's help for granted and not treating her with the respect she deserves as the woman that God has placed in his life to help him. Of course, logic tells us that if the man would fulfill his duties without needing constant reminders, his wife would not have anything to nag him about in the first place.

A wise woman can help a man keep balance in his life and not neglect his responsibilities in his home because he is spending too much time at work or in front of the computer or television. In many churches across the nation, sometimes it seems as if the pastor's wife is in control of the affairs of the church, as well as their husbands and many others within the congregation. She can appear bossy and pushy, but if you really look closely at the situation, you will see that she is just doing the part of the job that her husband tends to overlook and forget to do. That is how God uses her to make him more complete.

Many times it is hard for a true pastor to say no to a member, and he can easily overwork himself. He counsels even when he is hurting and stressed. Many times the first lady will step in to rescue her husband. She may encourage him to take a rest, and too often the congregation interprets this as meanness. Nothing could be further from the truth. She is always looking out for her husband when nobody else is. She will tell him to slow down because she sees him getting wrapped up in his job. She may seem harsh and lacking compassion at times, but she is just doing her job. A man who appreciates his wife's intervention will express his appreciation of her in private and in public. He certainly would not call her or regard her as a nag.

Saying that a wife's efforts to help is just a bunch of nagging is a form of disrespect that somehow seems to give the husband permission to ignore his wife's suggestions. But why, for example, have a brand new car and a new motor bike in front of your house when inside the house you have broken furniture, a door that is falling off the hinges, no money in the bank and no way to send your children to college? If her husband had been listening, he would have heard her question his reasons for purchasing expensive items when so many essential needs had been left unmet. When a man truly listens, he will make sure his wife has what she needs and is treated with respect.

A genuine relationship is built on honesty and respect. Patronizing, insincere remarks like "Yes, Dear" or "Yes, Honey" or "Anything you want, Honey" are the ingredients for a superficial relationship that does not have much sustenance. When a husband tells his wife what he thinks she wants to hear in order to make her feel good, the marital relationship is littered with deception and disrespect. But if a husband is committed to carving out a relationship that is genuine, mutual trust will grow and listening to one another will become easier and even more enjoyable.

7

MUM'S THE WORD

If you happen to be a man who claims that you would listen if only your wife would talk to you, I encourage you to check the atmosphere before you make any more sweeping assumptions. I say this because more often than not, if the wife does not like to speak with her husband, it is usually because he dominates and intimidates her. In most cases, she would talk if the man would make the environment safe for her to do so.

Another atmosphere that is not conducive for her a woman to talk is one in which she has given up trying because she long ago realized that he is not interested in what she has to say. Either he has tried to hurry her up so he can move on to something that interests him more, or he has mocked her, or interrupted her with his own sweeping opinions. A woman who has experienced this over a long time may have become bound up in fear or in anger and frustration.

Even if his woman has shut down because he has mistreated her or disregarded her in the past, he can woo her back to himself. One way to do this is showing genuine interest in some aspect of her life, like showering her with flowers and gifts, doing things for her when she least expects it, giving her praise, or romancing her with her with hugs and kisses. More than likely, he will pry that door open little by little and she will begin to believe the he values her. When this happens, the atmosphere for honest and authentic communication begins to be restored.

More than likely, she will begin to look for ways to captivate her husband and to bring happiness to him whenever she is around. Genesis 29:11 says that when Jacob was in the presence of Rachel he kissed her and began to weep aloud. He was excited to see her. Apart from his relationship with Jesus Christ, a man's wife should bring him the greatest joy. A wife is a husband's spice, aroma and fragrance; his season and his salt. She is his help and his enhancement. If her husband creates an atmosphere in which she feels free and encouraged to do so, she will bring delight to their marriage and design their home to be a haven of rest.

8
SENSITIVITY TO THE SPIRIT

Men are the strength of the church, while women are the emotions of the church—a trait that causes most women to be even more sensitive to the Spirit of God than most men. A woman usually can get into the flow of the Spirit more quickly during a worship service than a man can. This is because her unique sensitivity will usually take her into the arms of God much more quickly. I think women's added sensitivity to the Spirit is the real reason why most intercessors are women. And if the truth be told, their intercession is often what is keeping their husbands out of harm's way.

Like me, you may have noticed that it is much easier for a man to ask a woman to pray for him than it is for him to ask another man to pray for him. Even in that, we men have an intuitive sense that we should listen to a woman who has wisdom and knowledge. Knowing this, why not look for ways to receive from your wife's sensitivities to the Spirit and learn to flow with her in an unhindered way?

9

A LITTLE TLC

en must begin to understand how women relate to others. I thought my wife used to embarrass me until I realized it was only her sensitivity shining forth. She used to come into the house while I was having company and immediately ask them if they needed something to drink. I had been sitting with them for two or three hours and hadn't thought to ask if they were thirsty, but she walked in the door and instantly recognized that our company needed something to drink. I learned that the best way to not get embarrassed was to immediately ask my guests when they come to my house if they would like something to drink.

Another way that some men are embarrassed is when they ask a best friend to come over for dinner, and the friend shows up with flowers or a gift for his wife. It makes the man of the house think: "Why did he bring gifts for my wife? Doesn't he know that he is really messing up my day?" It sometimes takes another man to show the husband what he should have been doing all along. If you happen to be a man who keeps getting shown up by your friends, then by all means, learn a lesson and give your wife what she needs.

Some men complain that their wives live as if they were single women. I would challenge that type of comment from those men. First of all, Genesis 3:16 says that the desire of the woman will be for her husband. It is natural for a woman to want to have a loving family with a husband and children. However, when a married woman lives as if she is single, it is because the man is there in body and not in mind; he shows no commitment and does not communicate with her. Most men believe that their being around should be good enough for their wives. But when the man is always in the house and cannot even find time to go to the park or take a trip with his family, it becomes a problem. Some men even find it hard to spend money on their families without complaining. This causes some women to take the initiative to call up a friend and make plans to travel alone or buy themselves roses or go to the mall.

Women like that refuse to be discouraged and believe in living life to the fullest, refusing to live with depression in their marriages. Men must realize that their wives are their counterparts; they are there to help them, not to fight with them. Consider the example of Aquila and Priscilla in Acts 18. They worked together as a ministry team though they also were married. This is the kind of unity God desires for couples.

Many women are also having a hard time functioning on the job because they lack unity and the benefits of teaming in life with their husbands. If these women are forced to row the boat alone for too long, they may go into a personal survival mode that hinders them from being able to tend well to their family's needs and their friendships with other women. If the burnout continues to take over their ability to function in a healthy way, their spiritual lives will suffer and their church attendance will begin to wane.

Many couples are stressed out, having no money, joy or peace. They are simply living together in body and not in the unity of the spirit. This is why there are so many unsuccessful relationships today.

But this does not have to be their plight. First Peter 3:8 encourages couples to "live in harmony with each other." Couples can be of one mind and demonstrate such unity that it will release a blessing as they obey each other, loving each other so that both parties can receive the blessings they were called to inherit.

10

MAXIMIZE YOUR DAYS AND YOUR EMOTIONS

Psalm 90:12 says that we should "number our days," meaning we should pay attention to everything we do. That is one reason why God gives men a helper in their lives, to help point out things they do not see. This may even save his life. I say this because many men have unnecessarily died before their time. Once, I was told about a man who felt a little pain in his stomach but wouldn't listen when his wife asked him to go to the hospital. The pain got worse, and though he took several home remedies, the pain increased to the point that it drove him to the hospital. When the doctors examined him, they discovered that cancer had spread throughout his stomach, and he had no chance of survival. Had he listened to his wife, he might not have died this sudden death.

Certainly, some women can be overzealous, calling the doctor about every little thing. But many wives have saved their husbands' lives by encouraging them to get medical attention. In my experience, listening to my wife has even impacted my spiritual health and has had a tremendous impact on my ministry.

All too often husbands are just as resistant to other physical needs as they are to responding to their wives' prodding them to receive medical attention. When their husbands do not meet their need for viable communication and expressions of love, some married women begin to struggle with thoughts of committing adultery. Their lives seem to be stable—their homes are taken care of, their husbands and children are happy, and they are successful on their jobs—but they don't have the kind of close relationship with their husbands that they desire. The loss of their husband's attention has left them feeling undesirable and unloved. Just like the husband that does not recognize his need for emergency care in the hospital, he may miss the fact that his marriage is in serious trouble because he is missing his wife's spoken and unspoken heart cries.

For many of these women, marriage simply did not fulfill their girlhood fantasies. They have found themselves in relationships with childish men who refuse to grow up. They cry out for help, but no one seems to hear. When they attempt to talk with their husbands, they find them emotionally dull and lacking in understanding. So they struggle in secret, full of guilt and tormented about how they got to such a place.

I imagine there are thousands of wives crying out in homes because they don't feel cherished. Men, remember that the Bible says a man who loves his wife loves himself (see Ephesians 5:28). A man can get so busy that he no longer hears his wife's cries. Jesus responded to the needs and concerns of his mother, Mary. In John 2, when she asked Him for help when there was no more wine at a wedding feast, Jesus did as she requested, even though His hour had not yet come. It would have been embarrassing for the young couple to run out of wine at a prestigious occasion like a wedding. By listening and responding to Mary, Jesus saved the bride and groom from shame.

The same is true for couples. If men would listen to their wives even before they got to the place where they were crying out, they could save themselves and their wives from humiliation—in many cases from the shame of adultery, for example.

Listening to women as a means of avoiding shameful situations is not a new thing. In John 4, many men found salvation after listening to the testimony of the Samaritan woman. Even though she had prostituted herself, men in her community found eternal life because they listened to her. In 2 Samuel 20:14–22 we read of a wise woman who helped Joab and his army defeat their enemy. Men, we must remember that women are not in our lives to compete with us, but to complete us.

In 2 Kings 4, the Bible talks about a wise woman's shame was removed and her house was blessed when she observed Elisha as he passed by her house. She suggested to her husband that they build the prophet a room and furnish it for him. I don't know if her husband was happy with the idea, but eventually the room was built. Because of her generosity, Elisha asked her if there was anything she needed. The couple was childless and desired to have a baby, so the prophet told her she would have a baby the following year. In those days, being childless was a shameful thing. Because of her sensitivity to Elisha's needs, the woman received a blessing that removed her shame and fulfilled the deep desire of her and her husband's hearts.

Though the husband was the head of the house, in this case, he was not the one who discerned the prophet's needs. However, because he listened to his wife, the couple was blessed. I wonder how many couples have missed out on God's blessings because the husband refused to pay attention to his wife's suggestions. I am reminded of a man who is now successful in real estate because he purchased a property at his wife's recommendation. At first he was determined not to buy; the economy was down, prices were rising and he didn't think the timing was right. But he listened to his wife when she suggested that they buy the property, and now its value has gone through the roof. I don't have to tell you how glad he is that he listened to her.

I also recall a time when I was troubled about my child moving from preschool to elementary school, because of the influence this new school would have on my baby. My wife suggested that I attend the orientation meeting, but I didn't feel like sitting through an hour of talking so I made every excuse not to go. I thought that as long as my wife went, I didn't have to be there. Keep in mind that I was the one with the major concern.

Finally, I dropped all of my excuses, humbled myself and attended the meeting with my wife. After sitting through the orientation, I was at peace about the school. I found out the principle was saved; she even talked about a parenting series I was using at the church. I thank God I listened to my wife and attended that meeting. It completely relieved my concerns. Had I not gone, I'd probably still be worried and bringing my stress into my home.

I wonder why we men find it so difficult to trust our wives. Is it pride, even though the Bible says the woman is the glory of man (see 1 Corinthians 11:7)? The anointing that is on the man should also be on his wife. If you can speak into your wife's life, why can't you listen to her advice? It is like a student correcting the teacher about something taught in class. How would either of them grow if the teacher were too proud to take correction?

People are awarded for their athletic ability or other

achievements, but society does not give commendation for listening, even though listening is what enables us to be successful in all other things. Imagine how much disappointment we would avoid if we simply learned to listen well.

Many people are surprised that a man would write a book that explains the needs of women and how to understand them. I have learned a great deal from my wife as I have learned how to listen. She began to get my attention by asking if we could meet at a certain time to discuss a particular issue. That allowed me to prepare myself mentally and emotionally for what she wanted to share. It is not easy for men to listen if they are preoccupied with job stress or other distractions. From experience I can say that a man will be much more apt to listen to his woman if she also listens to him and remains sensitive to his needs.

In one of my previous books, *Push Beyond Your Pain: How to Survive Your Wilderness Experience,* I talk about my life story. I used to be very insensitive to women—so unfeeling, in fact, that I didn't even realize women had feelings until I was twenty-seven years old. After I got married, I realized that women had needs. As I became attentive to my wife's needs and learned how to truly love her, our marriage was strengthened. But I had to listen. My wife taught me what a woman wants and how she desires to be treated—how she needs to feel loved and fulfilled.

Responding to my wife in a way that made her feel cherished also impacted the intimacy in our relationship. If her husband isn't intimidated or uncomfortable about the conversation, a wife will tell him what pleases her sexually. Many married women are depressed about their sex lives because they don't feel fulfilled in the bedroom. They don't feel emotionally connected to their husbands, and they don't experience climax.

Proverbs 5:19 urges men to be ever captivated by their wives' love, to let their breasts satisfy them always. Philippians 2:3 tells us to esteem others better than ourselves. No man or woman should feel unfulfilled in the bedroom. Christian couples especially should experience the greatest joy in their sex lives. Those who desire a better sex life must be willing to change their own expectations of what will occur. This is accomplished when each party enters the bedroom with a readiness to please his or her spouse in ways that make him or her most comfortable. Doesn't the Bible say that it is more blessed to give than to receive?

First Corinthians 7 says that when a man is married he thinks of his wife and how to please her, and when a woman is married she thinks about her husband and how to please him. When couples become consumed with pleasing each other when they are making love, they are free of expectations and able to enjoy each other most freely. Couples should not be limited to a rote activity that is just another part of marriage. When Proverbs 5:19 says that a man should be "ravished" with his wife (KJV), it speaks of being filled with strong emotion and delight. Sex should not be a selfish act. If it is all that it was created to be, it will be an expression of a husband and wife's love for each other.

For this kind of exchange to be meaningful, it must be a form of two-way communication as well. It is easy to see that good communication in other areas of life will carry over into the bedroom and vice versa. The Song of Solomon gives a dialogue between two lovers, and the man is clearly captivated by his beloved. In chapter 4 the lover says his beloved has "stolen his heart" (see verse 9). If a woman wants her husband to be sexually motivated, she must be desirable to him. She must present herself in an attractive way. Husbands don't usually like to see their wives in nightclothes all day, wearing a "do rag" on their heads.

A man's relationship with his wife is one of the closest he will ever have with another human being. Even men who are very successful, with prosperous friends, say they can be most honest with their wives. The intimate relationship God desires a couple to share extends far beyond the bedroom. Many times wives carry their husbands' burdens in terms of decision-making. In times of crisis, a man needs to be able to lean on his spouse and glean from her wisdom.

Wives must pray fervently for wisdom to know how to respond to their husbands, especially during difficult seasons. A woman who exercises godly wisdom will be able to speak life into the situation and encourage her spouse. Wives, sometimes you will need to hang up the phone or put your agenda aside to give your husband the attention he needs. God wants you and your husband to work together as a team, and life's tests and trials can help bring you to a place of greater unity.

The book of Genesis paints a picture of Adam and Eve as a team in the Garden of Eden, exercising dominion together. Behind many millionaires, successful athletes and businessmen are faithful women who spoke into their lives before most others saw their potential.

Once while I was at the gym, I struck up a conversation with a guy who happened to be a Christian. My phone rang in the middle of our conversation, and it was my wife. The man mentioned that he shuts his phone off when he comes to the gym, because he doesn't want to talk with his wife. I leave my phone on when I am there, because I want my wife to be able to reach me in case of an emergency.

I sensed he had a problem with that, and I told him about the book I was working on, *Man, Listen to Your Woman*. He became irate and walked away, saying he did not want to hear that. We were having a good conversation until I told him about my book.

The fact that many men are so offended by the title of this book is a good indicator that their relationships with their wives are handicapped. The radical way in which they balk at the title also indicates to me that they are still in the place where I once was, lacking respect for women.

One passage of scripture that I have grown to love is in Judges 4 and 5. Here, we read about how God used the prophetess Deborah and of a man who was not ashamed to cooperate with a woman in a way that would strike right at the heart of many men's inflated egos. She encouraged Barak, who led an Israelite coalition to victory over the militarily superior Canaanite forces. The exploit landed Barak in Hebrews 11, among the great heroes of the faith. Though Deborah is not mentioned, it is clear that Barak could not have won the battle without her. Barak and Deborah were not married, but this is another illustration of how true the saying is that behind every great man there's a great woman.

The Canaanite army was many times greater than the army of Israel, but Deborah instructed Barak to go into battle. Barak, who was a general, listened to the Spirit of God that was flowing through Deborah. Barak told Deborah that if she would go with him then he would go. But if she refused to accompany him, he would not proceed into battle. Barak was not scared and weak; he had a huge responsibility on his shoulders and wanted to make a wise decision.

As in the case of Deborah and Barak, even the strongest, most capable leader can benefit from having wise counsel, and sometimes God will bring a woman into his life to provide that insight. Husbands can look at it this way: No matter how great a position you hold as a man, you still need your wife's help to win many of the victories in life. Without, your success in your marriage and in other aspects of your life will hampered. Barak put aside his pride and submitted himself to the Spirit of God that was operating in Deborah—and she led them into great victory over the enemy.

When you are really in need of help, you cannot afford to be a skeptic or prejudiced. If Barak had allowed pride to rule his life, he wouldn't have been able to sense God directing him through Deborah. Barak promised to go only if Deborah went. It was not that he was fearful and wanted to hide behind Deborah's skirt. He had confidence in the direction she would give him. Oh, if only more of us men would learn the value of interdependence, cooperation, and teamwork with the woman that God has uniquely gifted to help us. But just as I learned a little later in life than some, it's never to late to begin.

11

BALANCING ACTS

When two people come together who are opposite—let's say one is emotional and the other stoic—they have the potential to help balance each other out. If the man allows the woman's emotions to help soften his hardness, she may become less emotionally driven and be able to see the more practical aspects of certain issues. Both the man and the woman benefit from the balance that each brings to the other.

A woman who has been doing all of the giving and all of the attempting to bring balance to the relationship will lose some of the emotional stability that she once had. When she has been rowing the boat by herself for too long because the husband has stopped contributing to the health of the relationship, she may give up, shut up, or sink into depression. This is not the time for a husband to respond to his wife in hardness. It is time to put gentleness into overdrive.

To do this in an authentic way, try to remember what you used to do that first attracted her. She once thought you were the greatest thing to walk on two feet. When something is neglected for a long time, it is difficult to start fresh. But your relationship with your spouse is worth the effort. Your wife needs tender loving care. Call her at work sometimes. Send flowers to her job. Remember to ask her how her day was. Try to be sensitive to the things that interest her. If she keeps saying her body aches, buy some oil and give her a massage. If she gets tired of the kids and the stresses at home, take the family out for a ride and give her some time to herself. Your marriage is worth it. If you start rowing the boat once again, before long her hope and strength will return and she will begin rowing in sync with you.

12

GIVE THE WOMEN A BREAK

I was motivated to write this section while on a road trip during a week-long revival. I had never preached at this particular church and had decided to bring along a singing group called the Morgan Sisters. These sisters were highly respected singers who had sung in some major venues. They had ministered all over the country to thousands of people and had opened many different shows for people such as Alvin Slaughter, BeBe and CeCe Winans and Phil Driscoll.

Everything was fine until the third night of the revival. I had asked one of the deacons where the Morgan Sisters would be singing, assuming the whole time that they would minister from the pulpit. Boy, was I wrong. After all these women had accomplished and how much they had blessed the church with their music, the church refused to allow them to sing in the pulpit simply because they were women. This is what I call a plain lack of knowledge of the Word.

To make matters worse, this all happened shortly after the terrorist attack on September 11, 2001. Media reports were circulating about the repressive treatment of Afghani women, and one would think that sort of thing would not happen here. But I discovered that many churches in the United States were similarly repressive; they just did it in the name of Christ.

Nowhere in Scripture does Jesus make women feel inferior to men or ever deny a woman from hearing his preaching or getting close to Him. As a matter of fact, Jesus was criticized for being welcoming of women. In the midst of one of His sermons, a prostitute walked past more "respectable" people in the crowd and made her way to the pulpit to the feet of Jesus. Never did He tell her to step back so He could lay hands on her in the pew.

A pulpit is what you make it, but we have become much like the Pharisees in Matthew 23. They worshiped the altar instead of the God of the altar. Your pulpit can be a sidewalk, a kitchen, a living room or even a bathroom, but the pulpit has been used to isolate women, many of whom are called, gifted and anointed. Too many Christians, particularly men, force a double standard on women. They believe they are good enough to sing a solo, give their time to clean the church and raise funds for the ministry, yet they are not good enough to put their feet on a manmade altar in the church.

The modern church is not the temple of old, where there was the inner court, outer court and the most holy place. Christ has torn down the wall of separation so we can come in and out as we please. There is no Greek or Jew, bond or free, male or female, but we are all one in Christ Jesus and must be treated as one (see Galatians 3:8; Colossians 3:11).

I will now say something that will shock some of these modern-day Pharisees who are holding women down: If the women left the church, there would no longer be a church to go to. The women are motivators. They motivate their husbands, the pastor, the deacon and the young people. They are not just ushers, water carriers or nursery workers. They are the backbone of the church. There are more women in the church than there are men, and many of these women give so much to the church that their husbands complain even though dinner is always on the table and their needs are always met.

I wish women would get the credit they deserve in the church. The pastors and deacons celebrate the success of the church, but they often forget the women who helped make it possible. Even when we are celebrating the pastor's anniversary, I often give all the credit to my wife for encouraging me to reach this far and for being my burden-bearer. Just like a good woman is always behind a good man, a group of good women is behind every successful church.

The women's influence is even seen in the financial stability of the church. In some cases, it is because their husbands only give to the church because their wives challenge them to do so. In other cases, it is because the women of the church have supported ministries across this country with their best, even if it was the last dollar or meal they had to offer. These women are much like the woman in Mark 12:41–44 who gave her last small coins to Jesus; and the widow at Zarephath in 1 Kings 17:8–15 who gave her last cake of bread to the prophet Elijah even though she thought that she and her son were doomed to die.

So much that a woman does goes unnoticed, both in the church and in the home. She will tell her husband how good he looks and how strong and muscular he is, even though he has no muscles. She continues to get her hair done, even though he doesn't notice.

The double standards for women are everywhere. Some men threaten to leave their wives if they gain weight, but if a man becomes fat, his wife will usually stay with him and love him the same. Too often women pay more for cars, clothes and haircuts—even when they go to the same barber as men. Give the women a break!

They work harder and get paid less, and when it is time

to celebrate, they get shuffled to the back. Even in the church, the leadership sets up rules and twist Scriptures in order to dominate women. Many pastors don't support women preachers, though in Joel 2:28 God said He would pour out His Spirit on all flesh, that our sons and daughters would prophesy. If men will not assume their role to preach, women will do it, and they will do a great job.

Discrimination limits us from our greatest potential. Women must not subject themselves to second-class citizenship within the church. Together, men and women must look at the Spirit of God in these women and lead the way to liberate them.

The Bible says in Titus 2:5 that the woman should be the keeper of the home. After walking a mile in my wife's shoes, I've learned that this is no easy job. After our first child was born, my wife went to work and I stayed home with the baby. I had no idea what she went through as the caretaker of our home until I experienced it myself. As time went on and we had more children, I learned how to juggle. I had to change a four-month-old's diaper as my two-year-old pulled at my leg wanting something to eat as the phone rang with someone from the church seeking counsel. On any given day, I would make formula for the baby, clean the house and drop the oldest child off at school. I remember thinking, "I can't wait for my wife to come home from work so I can drop everything in her lap and run out the door and escape the pressure."

I thank God I didn't have to carry the children for nine months. That's a responsibility no mother can shirk. She has to carry her own weight. Until we men walk a mile in our wives' shoes, we won't know what they go through. In the home, in the church and on the job—men, give the women a break!

13

RESTORING BROKEN MEN

As I travel around the country, preaching and sharing my testimony, men often approach me and tell me that they want to know how to be made whole and move to the next level. Some of them seem to have their lives all together—they wear fine clothes, drive a nice car and live in a fancy house. But they are lost in a cave and cannot find their way out. John 5:1–6 tells of a man who laid at the pool of Bethesda for thirty-eight years, waiting for a miracle. Finally his time came to be delivered.

This man is not named in Scripture, so I am going to call him the broken man. He can represent anyone; just put your name in the space of his. Jesus asked the man, "Do you want to be whole?" Like Christ wanted to make this man whole, He wants to make you whole. Making you whole involves more than just healing. It requires restoration as well. It is clear in Scripture that God wants to give His children more than a temporary fix. Psalm 23:3 lets us know that God is a restorer of broken people, not just a healer of our flesh. And Psalm 84:11 says God will not withhold any good thing from those who walk uprightly. In Isaiah 1:18–19 the Bible says those who are willing and obedient will eat the good of the land. God wants you to have life and have it more abundantly ("to the full"; see John 10:10), and He explains how in His Word.

The man at the pool of Bethesda had been there so

long, he had probably had his fill of pain and rejection and was ready to be made whole. In order for change to occur in any life, the person has to want to be healed. Deuteronomy 30:19 puts it plainly: "I set before you life and death, blessings and curses. Now choose life." Why would any man or woman settle for a broken life?

It is difficult for a broken man to offer stable leadership. Usually the wife of a broken man will become hardened and bitter because of the way her husband treats her. She pent up her emotions because her husband is so bound up that she consider tears to be foolish. Could it be because the husband does not want to confess his need for healing and restoration? A broken man who unleashes his suffering upon on his wife, the bone of his bone and the flesh of his flesh, will only increase his own suffering.

A woman who is with a broken man may find that he is afraid to commit to her. He may live with her for years without wanting to marry her. The woman sticks around, holding on to a hope that will never materialize. She may even have children, but often even that does not force a broken man to offer her more stability.

There are many other symptoms of brokenness. The man may get angry when his wife or live-in girlfriend gets upset about something that he knows he has done wrong. Instead of facing the problem, he gets offended—his brokenness coming through. A person who is whole or mature takes responsibility for his or her wrong.

Women must be very careful when they marry or are dating a man from a broken environment. They will need great wisdom and discernment if they are to navigate these trouble waters without suffering too much harm.

This does not mean that God cannot make a broken man whole again. Look at Moses. In the book of Exodus we see that Moses was trained by the society of Egypt and later committed murder, but God healed him and used him to perform great miracles and to lead Israel out of captivity. Jacob was a trickster who deceived his brother, Esau, out of his birthright and his blessing (see Genesis 27). But in Genesis 32, we see Jacob wrestling with God—an encounter that changed him forever. However, a person who wants to be made whole must be willing to fight for it. You see, just like brokenness did not come overnight, healing and restoration are almost sure to come gradually.

The book of Job says a man's way is hidden (see 3:23), which means we need the direction of the Holy Ghost to lead us. God is willing to help. Philippians 2:13 says that God works in us to "act according to his good purpose." It is God's will for every broken man to be healed and made whole. However, this too is a two-way process. A man must do his part in this as well. God will be able to work in the heart of a man who cries out for help. Healing and restoration is sure to be gained by a man who is willing to see his own pride and arrogance and to allow the Master Potter to put him back together.

Those who remain broken may become like Ahab. In 1 Kings 21, we see the Samarian king lose control of his house and allow his wife, Jezebel, to make all the decisions. He had no backbone and brought a curse upon his house. Though many men can be manipulative in their homes, brokenness can cause others to relinquish all authority and seem schizophrenic in their decision-making. This frustrates the women in their lives because they do not always know how to deal with the frequent mood swings. As the women try to respond to their husbands' fluctuations from one emotional state to another, they begin to feel like they are living with six different men and never know who will be showing up next.

The burden to change the man, however, does not rest on the shoulders of his woman. Change will come when he takes an honest look at himself and spends quality time in God's Word and in prayer, learning the truth about how God sees him and what plans God has for him.

No woman really wants a man with no backbone. But she will step in and fill the position if the man fails to. A broken man who becomes whole will enrich everyone around him. His blessing of restoration will not be his alone. His wife will have a man who is whole enough to stand tall, strong enough to protect her, and mature enough to love her.

14

WOMAN, LISTEN TO YOUR MAN

Communication works both ways. Even though the title of this book is *Man, Listen to Your Woman*, there is also a need for a woman to listen to her man. Wives, if your husband is trying to communicate with you, listen to him. Men may appear very strong and tough, but they have feelings too. Just as a woman who is ignored again and again may stray physically or emotionally, the same is true of a man. If his wife won't listen to him and is always critical of him, a man could be led astray by a woman who will hear him out and affirm his efforts. Don't send your husband into another woman's arms.

For instance, if your husband tells you a specific thing that you do that dishonors him, listen to him and respond to what he is saying. Women are said to have long memories, bringing up things that happened long ago. But men can have a hard time letting things go too, especially in areas where they have suffered embarrassment. If he comes up against a brick wall whenever he expresses a need for you to change in a particular area, eventually he will withdraw from his wife and walk through a more open and softer door. Generally, women forgive more easily than men. It is more likely for a woman to take a man back who has cheated on her than for a man to take a woman back who has cheated. It's not fair, but that's the way it is.

This also holds true for the husband who talks with his wife about something he dislikes that is an area of weakness for her. A woman who discusses the issue with her husband and assesses with him what can be done to resolve the issue will grow with her husband instead of apart from him.

It is important for a woman to keep in mind that men are not like most women; they will tell another woman their problems before they tell another man. Just as there are men who prey on vulnerable women, there are also women who seek out vulnerable men. Such a woman will discern his weakness and make her move. She may be a polite, kindhearted coworker, or a cute woman from the neighborhood who seems to be successful. All she needs to do is be there when a man's heart is heavy.

The Bible says in Proverbs 21:9 that it is better to live on the corner of a rooftop than in a house with a quarrelsome woman. A woman can chase a man away with her sharp tongue long before she locks him out of his own house or he walks away, determined to never return again.

This usually happens when the woman neither values the man nor what he has to say. However, a woman who holds dear to her man will listen for subtle hints that will help her determine how to draw him out and bring the issues of his heart closer to hers. This woman will recognize that because men communicate differently, one word can be a very key to understanding what he is venturing to say. Because that one word may be like hidden gem, one that he did not even call attention to by stressing it, a wise and loving wife will listen carefully for the clues to the treasures of his heart. She will also carefully explore possible ways for her to lighten his load and initiate changes that will bring him added joy and peace.

15

LORD, TEACH ME HOW TO LOVE MY WIFE

If you ask most men if they love their wives, they will say they do. On the other hand, if you ask most women if their husbands love them, they would probably say yes, but their husbands don't express their love in the way they would like. Most men express love by providing for their families—doing their best to give their wives and children what they want. He would die doing so.

However, that is not the only way a woman desires to have love expressed to her. She needs emotional support, to be touched, admired and complimented, which can sometimes bring conflict into a relationship. Although the man thinks he is doing his best by providing for her needs, his wife thinks he doesn't love her enough because he isn't being romantic. Misunderstandings like these often make men feel like failures.

For the most part, women want their men to express the love in multi-dimensional ways. Oftentimes, this is not all that easy for men to do because so many of us have grown up never hearing the words "I love you" from family members or loved ones. We were not taught how to express love. Many men may seem fit on the outside—with strong muscles and striking physiques—but their emotional muscles are underdeveloped. And because they have little training on how to express love, their wives are disappointed in how one-dimensional their love relationships with their husbands have turned out to be.

We can pray, however. In Psalm 27:11, David asked God to teach him His ways. It is the will of God for us to love our wives as Christ loves the church and gave Himself for it (see Ephesians 5:25). If a man desires to love his wife in this way, he can receive direction through praying to God and reading the Word. In Romans 5:5, the Bible says God has poured out His love into our hearts by the Holy Spirit, whom He has given us. Men, the Holy Spirit living in us can show us how to love our wives. We have not because we ask not. Pray that the gift of love that is in you will be stirred up for your wife. If you can express your feeling to her when you are being intimate, you can do it at other times.

A man can also gain concrete strategies by simply asking his wife what she wants from him and showing her in other ways that he wants to know what will help her to feel loved. This is where our manly pride comes in, because we do not want our wives to tell us how to love or treat them. This is also where there is another opportunity for us to reap the benefits of humbling ourselves.

In his book *The Four Loves,* C. S. Lewis mentions these kinds of love—*agape* (the love of God), *storge* (the love of family), *phileo* (brotherly love) and *eros* (sexual love).[1] Most men love their wives through *eros* and *phileo* love, but we rarely achieve *agape* love. And that's how the devil sometimes gets into our relationships. *Agape* love helps us to love our wives beyond their faults and to see their potential. We must remember that, through the help of the Holy Spirit, we can do all things. First John 2:27 tells us that the Holy Spirit is our teacher, and He can show us how to love our wives because He is love. But being taught requires that we acknowledge where we are falling short.

I talked about three components of love and suggested

loving our wives through the *agape* love, which is a more effective way to love her unconditionally. These three types of love make up a threefold cord, which Ecclesiastes 4:12 says is not easily broken. To understand a threefold cord, we must look at how it is joined together and twisted. The chords are intertwined so that there is no space between them. Now imagine that you, your wife and God are wrapped tightly together in love as a three-fold cord. If you want to love your wife, you must keep God first in your life. The mistake many couples make is that when they join in holy matrimony, they squeeze God out of their relationships after a time, yet they expect the love of God to prevail in their marriages.

Colossians 3:15 tells us that when the peace of God rules our hearts, it also rules our relationships. In other words, do not get too busy for church, men; after all, you can only give to your wife what you receive from spending time in the presence of God. If you keep your love for God strong, your love for your wife will also remain strong. You can't increase your love for someone if you do not spend time with him or her. For example, the way a man's children react to him is a good way to tell how much time he spends with them. This is also true of how a husband and wife respond to one another. How can a couple grow closer to each other if they have separate bedrooms?

How beautiful it is to turn over in bed and see your wife sleeping there—even if she snores or her eyes and mouth are half open when she sleeps! When she wakes up, you can joke about it. Things like this will draw you closer together.

Showing your wife how much you love her can begin with telling her how you truly feel about her. You may not be able to verbalize your emotions like she does, but you can start do your best and be confident that with practice, you will grow in this area. You can express your love to her in other ways too. You can tell her how good she looks, ask how her day went, take her out for dinner, go through old photos together, go shopping with her, visit your in-laws with her—it doesn't matter where you start, just start somewhere.

When expressing love is especially hard, it may indicate that we are holding a grudge against our spouse. Many people who do not respect their spouses and show them love are actually secretly bitter toward them. If bitterness has its hold on you, draw close to God and to your wife and seek the help you need to forgive and let go of the offense. A husband and a wife who are quick to apologize to each other will be helping to ensure that bitterness does not take root and choke out their ability to express love toward one another.

John 3:16 describes love in action. If we know to do good and do not do it, we sin. Love is not only a matter of what we say, but also of what we do.

If a man does not seek to love his wife in the way that he should, he will have ongoing temptations to be unfaithful—whether that infidelity is carried out physically or mentally. The Bible says we should be satisfied with our wives and ravished with her love (see Proverbs 5:19, KJV). This will make it harder for intruders to come in and weaken the relationship.

A lifetime of exploration of how to love one another awaits you. As you do one to another, eagerly respond to the other's needs and empower one another to reach your destinies, you will be tending the garden of your love well and be ravished by its fruit forever.

16
MARRIED BUT STILL LONELY

Oftentimes the woman reflects what the man gives her—whether love, depression or frustration. The enemy can easily use this to his advantage by attacking the man and using him against his wife, especially if he struggles with pride or is not sensitive to her needs. Insensitivity is a fertile breeding ground for loneliness.

In some cases, a wife will allow herself to only reflect what she feels to the status of her relationship with her husband. But this does not have to be the case. A woman can choose to reflect her close relationship with the Lord instead. Most high-profile husbands are just hardworking men trying to meet the demands of life. They do not consciously neglect their wives and kids. So most of these wives find themselves competing with their husbands' career as they seek his love and attention. By casting her cares on the Lord and depending on Him to supply what she needs, a woman can avoid the ramifications of being in a constant state of disappointment and loneliness.

Sometimes wives get so dependent on their husbands that they can forget God. In many relationships, husbands and wives are secure in their careers, homes and families. They are living the American dream, yet they experience deep frustration and loneliness that are actually the result of a breakdown in their spiritual walk with God.

Any time people try to do anything without God, they

are setting themselves up for disappointment. God wants everyone—married or single—to be completely dependent and submitted to Him. God wants to satisfy our every longing. If we learn to be satisfied in Him, we can still be happy even when our spouses are not there. Sometimes you have to create your own environment of happiness when your spouse is not around because you are not putting the purposes of God in front of your own desires. This is a mark of maturity in a marital relationship.

Living for the sole purpose of trying to please another person can also result in loneliness. A wife whose only concern is to please her husband will not ask for what she needs. Doesn't James 4:2 tell us that we have not because we ask not. If a woman wants her husband to hug her, to sit with her, to kiss her or to simply spend time with her, she must tell him. Being in her presence in no way guarantees that he will know what she needs. If she does not tell him, and her needs go unmet, she will ultimately suffer loneliness, frustration and burnout. The husband may not respond to his wife's requests right away because he is so used to her doing all of the emotional work, but over time he will probably begin to process, understand and respond to what she is saying.

In summation, the ultimate Source for our needs is suppose to be God. He, however, has designed marriage as a way of fulfilling some of those needs. And like we are to ask God in prayer for what we need, couples are to stay within the safeguard of telling one another what their needs are and doing their best to provide for them. A couple also treads on dangerous ground when they are not physically intimate with one another. God commands couples to refrain from being intimate only during fasting (see 1 Corinthians 7:3–5). Husbands and wives are safeguarding their marriages when they are on guard for any hurt, anger or unforgiveness that would impede them from coming together in the marriage bed. They are also protecting their marriage when they work at being attractive to their spouse and make their spouse feel desirable.

Failure to address loneliness will not make it go away. Couples who deal with issue by talking about it and making sure their priorities are in order will help ensure that they will avoid its pitfalls.

Singles would do well to consider carefully why they want to get married. Marriage is not the answer to loneliness. Men and women alike must learn how to be happy and content by themselves so they can go into a relationship complete and whole—because when two people are married and not getting along, the loneliness will become even greater.

If a couple enters a marriage as two lonely, broken individuals, there will be twice as much depression, twice as much loneliness and twice as much frustration. The most frustrating part of the relationship will be that there will be a person in the house but now loneliness is haunting you both even more. That's why some married people think they would be better off alone. This line of reasoning leads to divorce, as it seems easier to drop the weight to relieve the pressure.

The key to peace and happiness in your relationship is to pray and to quickly respond to your spouse's areas of loneliness. If not addressed, the loneliness will spread to another part of your home, even to your children.

A husband can be likened to a faucet, and his wife to a container that holds the water from the faucet. If the container is empty, it is because the faucet has been turned off. The end result will be drought in the home. A lonely wife breeds a lonely home, a happy wife a happy home. When the husband chooses to turn on the life force in his home—his wife and children are replenished. A man is not responsible for all his wife's happiness, but a man may have a lonely wife because he is not doing all he can do.

Psalm 101:2 says, "I will be careful to lead a blameless life—when will you come to me? I will walk in my house with blameless heart." Close relationships have great potential for conflict. Our family members usually see us at our worst because we relax and let down our mask of good behavior. Often we do not treat our relatives with the same respect and kindness we show to friends and business associates. The psalmist David must have understood this as he promised to walk within his house with a perfect heart. Why would we not do our best to treat those closest to us well? Why would we want not strive to be Christian examples of grace and peace in our own homes?

When God puts two people together, He gives them a measure of grace to deal with each other. But when those two people move beyond God's boundaries for them, they will not experience God's best for them. Because God often puts together two people who are opposite from another and complement one another, keeping God in the center of the marriage is critical in withstanding the test of time and flourishing. It is not always easy. Oftentimes, it requires us to stand firm and tall in our determination to be humble, submit to one another and walk in truth and love.

As you ponder these nuggets of truth and matters of the heart, I encourage you to keep Nehemiah 4:14 in mind: Fight for your brothers, your sons and your daughters, your wives and your homes."

NOTES

Preface

1. Joshua Harris, *I Kissed Dating Goodbye* (Sisters, OR: Multnomah Publishers, 1997).

Chapter 15
Lord, Teach Me How to Love My Wife

1. C. S. Lewis, *The Four Loves* (New York: Harcourt, 1960).